CHRISTMAS
Merrymaking

Christ Child
Vintage postcard
Czechoslovakia, postally used 1921

CHRISTMAS
Merrymaking

Barbara Hallman Kissinger

PELICAN PUBLISHING COMPANY

GRETNA 2007

The word "Pelican" and the depiction of a pelican are trademarks
of Pelican Publishing Company, Inc., and are registered in the
U.S. Patent and Trademark Office.

Library of Congress Cataloging-in-Publication Data

Kissinger, Barbara Hallman.
  Christmas merrymaking / by Barbara Hallman Kissinger.
      p. cm.
  Includes bibliographical references.
  ISBN-13: 978-1-58980-482-1 (hardcover : alk. paper) 1. Christmas in art. 2. Christmas—
History. 3. Magazine illustration. 4. Illustration of books. 5. Postcards. I. Title.
    NC968.5.C45K568 2007
    760'.04493942663--dc22

                                         2007016426

Illustration on title page: *Vintage postcard*
made in Germany, postally used ca. 1910

Printed in Singapore
Published by Pelican Publishing Company, Inc.
1000 Burmaster Street, Gretna, Louisiana 70053

To my children:
Daniel, Tracy, Lori, Kyle, and Erin

Vintage postcard
Postally used 1908

Glædelig Jul

Vintage postcard marked EAS
Denmark, ca. 1908

CONTENTS

Vintage postcard
ca. 1912

A happy
Christmas.

*Vintage postcard marked B.W.
Printed in Germany, postally used
1906*

PROLOGUE

I have loved Christmas since I was four years old. On my fourth Christmas in 1937, Santa brought me a Tootsietoy® tin dollhouse full of metal furniture. I was so excited and delighted with my dollhouse. It is one of my earliest memories. What is your first joyous Christmas memory?

In the late 1970s, my mother gave me a book on Christmas and it piqued my interest in the history of the holiday season, and my collecting of Christmas ephemera began. My Christmas postcard collection started with Santas. I used them as research material to make wooden folk-art Santas that were historically correct to the period they represented. I sold the wooden Santas across the United States in the eighties and nineties. You can still find a few once in a while on Ebay.

It was during this time I started collecting more books, nineteenth and early twentieth century period

Vintage postcard marked EAS
Printed in Germany, postally used 1910

Vintage postcard
Printed in Germany, postally used 1909

Vintage postcard marked B.W. Christmas
Printed in Germany, ca. 1909

newspapers, and book and magazine illustrations pertaining in anyway to Christmas. I wanted to research anything that was related to the customs and traditions of Christmas past and the people that contributed to them. Within the last ten years I began thinking about doing a book on Christmas using my collection along with a text of Christmas history. In the fall of 2005 my first book *Christmas Past* was published. It was very well received, thanks to a lot of you.

This book, *Christmas Merrymaking,* is a continuation of the joys of *Christmas Past.* It is a picture book with many illustrations and vintage postcards of the Christmas season. The history in this book is taken from nineteenth and twentieth century books and from articles of the same period that accompanied some of the illustrations in my Christmas collection.

Christmas Merrymaking begins with a mention of why we celebrate Christmas, that is of course, the birth of Christ. It then covers the merrymaking and feasting of the holiday season in earlier centuries. Illustrations of Santa depict the progression of Santa's image in England and America. Last, but not least, *Christmas Merrymaking* shows you some of the beautiful (many German generated) postcards of the Christmas season in the early twentieth century. It is my deepest wish that you will enjoy *Christmas Merrymaking.*

So let us begin with the reason for the celebration of Christmas, the birth of Christ. This is what Christmas is all about.

Mary gave birth to Jesus. An angel came to announce the birth of our Savior to the shepherds. The shepherds went directly to visit the baby Jesus and then started spreading the word of the birth of the son of God. The Magi followed the Christmas Star and brought their gifts to the Christ child and worshiped him. These beautiful postcards tell the story.

This book also presents some of the history of Christmas that began in England.

Quite a few of these customs came to America and enhanced our traditions.

Vintage postcard marked B.W. 372
Printed in Germany, ca.1909

THOSE JOLLY CHRISTMAS DAYS IN

PICTURED BY ROBERT SEYMOUR, THE FAMOUS ENGLISH CARICATURIST

BRINGING
HOME
CHRISTMAS
GREENS

*"Forth to the wood
did merry men
go,
To gather in the
mistletoe."*

COMING HOME FROM SCHOOL

HEADS OF THE FAMILY

*"Let's dance and sing, and make good cheer,
For CHRISTMAS COMES BUT ONCE A YEAR!"*

THE BARONIAL HALL

*"All travellers, as they do pass on their way,
At gentlemen's halls are invited to stay,
Then come, boys, and welcome for diet the chief,
Plum-pudding, goose, capon, minc'd-pies, and
roast beef."*

A LONDON MARKET—CHRISTMAS EVE

CHRISTMAS PLUM PUDDING

STORY-TELLING
CHRISTMAS EVE

*A tale of bygone generations,
told by a withered crone
grown old in service.*

BRINGING IN THE
BOAR'S HEAD

THOSE WANDERING SPIRITS OF
HARMONY, THE WAITS

Those Jolly Christmas
Days in Merry England
of Long Ago

MERRIE ENGLAND OF LONG AGO

WHO CREATED FOR CHARLES DICKENS THE FIRST PICKWICK TYPE

"MERRY
CHRISTMAS
TO YOU!"

COUNTRY
CHURCH
CHRISTMAS
MORNING

*"And all the bells on
earth shall ring,
On Christmas-day in
the morning."*

THE NORFOLK COACH AT CHRISTMAS

CHRISTMAS
PANTOMIME

*"England was merry Eng-
land, when
Old Christmas brought his
sports again."*

TOO LATE FOR THE COACH

CHRISTMAS MUMMERS

*"Here come I, old Father Christmas, welcome, or welcome not,
I hope old Father Christmas will never be forgot."*

SNAPDRAGON

THE MISTLETOE BOUGH

*Tradition said that the maid who was not kissed under it,
at Christmas, would not be married in the next year.*

THE CHRISTMAS DINNER A CENTURY AGO

A gathering together of generations.

from The Ladies' Home
Journal, *December 1917*
Art by Robert Seymour

Vintage postcard, Series of Christmas,
Postcard No. 512, Raphael Tuck &
Sons
Printed in Saxony, postally used 1910

CHRISTMAS Merrymaking

Vintage postcard, ca. 1910

Vintage postcard, ca. 1910

Merrymaking

Christmas and His Children
from The Book of Christmas, *1888*
Frontispiece by Robert Seymour

Christmas, through the centuries, has been greatly celebrated especially in England. The engraving of "Vanity Fair," which is also the name of the festival in the early novel *Pilgrim's Progress,* by John Runyan, shows the extremes of the celebration of the times. The festival was described as a scene of frivolity and flamboyance. An entry from a lady's diary of 1684 describes the scene of the festival from the London Christmas and New Year of 1683-84.

The lady writes:

The frost continuing more and more severe, the Thames before London was still planted with booths in formal streets, all sorts of trades and shops furnished, and full of commodities, even to a printing-press, where the people and ladies took a fancy to have their names printed. This humor took so universally, that twas estimated the printer gained five pounds a day for a line only at sixpence a name, besides what he got for ballads, etc. Coaches plied from Westminster to the Temple, and from several other stairs to and fro, as in the street, sled, sliding with skates, a bull-baiting, horse and coach races, puppet-plays and interludes, cooks, tipling, and other lewd places, so that it seemed to be a bacchanalian triumph, or carnival on the water.

A bacchanalian celebration refers to Roman times when the Romans had several festivals for their god of wine—Bacchus. In the beginning they were held in secret by women only, later men joined the celebrations. It became a raucous time with orgies everywhere. The Roman Senate eventually banned the practice, but they continued in the south of Italy in private.

Henry VIII was King of England from 1509-1547. It was during his reign when the Christmas masque came into fashion. The illustration of Henry VIII depicts

Vanity Fair—Christmas 1683
from Graphic, Christmas Number December 25, 1876

him keeping Christmas and being entertained by a host of guests masked for the affair.

In the book *Christmas and Christmas Lore,* the author T. G. Crippen quotes the description of the masque from *The Masque of Christmas* by Ben Jonson:

First came *Father Christmas* with two or three of his guard, and a drum beaten before him. He wore a close doublet, round hose, long stockings cross-gartered, white shoes, a high-crowned hat with a brooch, and a little ruff; he had a long thin beard, and carried a truncheon. Then came his ten children, led in a string by Cupid, and each with a suitable attendant. *Misrule* wore a velvet cap with a sprig, a short cloak, and a great yellow ruff: his torch-bearer carried a basket with a cheese and a rope. *Carol* had a red cap and a long tawny coat, with a flute hanging at his girdle: his torch-bearer carried a song book, open. *Minced Pie* was neatly dressed as the cook's wife; her man carried a pie on a dish, and a spoon. *Gambol* appeared as a tumbler, with a hoop and bells; his torch-bearer was armed with a 'colestaff' and a blinding cloth. *Post and Pair* had a pair-royal of aces in his hat; his garment was done over with 'pairs and purs:' his squire carried a box with cards and counters. *New Year's Gift* was like a serving-man, in a blue coat, with an orange, and a sprig of rosemary gilt on his head; his hat is stuck full of brooches, and his collar is made of gingerbread: his

King Henry VIII Keeping Christmas at Greenwich
from The Illustrated London News, *December 19, 1863*
By John Gilbert

torch-bearer carries a 'marchpane' and a bottle of wine on each arm. *Mumming* wears a pied suit with a visor; his torch-bearer carries a box and rings it. *Wassail* is a neatly dressed maiden: her page bears a brown bowl, dressed with ribbons and rosemary, before her. *Offering* wears a short gown and carries a porter's staff; his torch-bearer goes before him with a basin and a wyth. Finally, *Baby-cock* is dressed like a little boy, in a fine long coat and a cap with ear-pieces, with bib, muck-ender, and a little dagger: his usher carries a great cake with a bean and a pea.

A Christmas masque was a sixteenth and seventeenth century intense and exciting bit of entertainment. In the Christmas masque illustration, "Christmas Masque at the Court of Charles II," the main character is Father Christmas or Old Christmas. Father Christmas is bringing in the steaming wassail bowl of spiced ale, which was used to toast to everyone's good health. All the characters of the masque are trailing behind him. Some of the participants are disguised as grotesque monsters or animals. These kinds of disguises came from the pagan custom of celebrating on the kalends of January. It was a Roman New Year's celebration. One can feel the merriment in this illustration with its characters performing for their king.

The custom of mumming had its roots in the Roman

Christmas Masque at the Court of Charles II
from The Illustrated London News, *December 24, 1859*

Mummers at Christmas in the Olden Time
from The Illustrated London News, *December 22, 1866*
By E. N. Corbould

celebration called Saturnalia, which started December 17th and lasted for a week. During this celebration, men and women exchanged clothing and participated in wild merrymaking. The mummers in wild disguises would go from house-to-house or court-to-court, partaking in the Christmas cheer and merriment.

The illustration "Mummers at Christmas in the Olden Time" is a depiction of a scene, during the reign of Henry II in the twelfth century, of a lord being entertained by the mummers in his ancestral hall. The hall is adorned with tapestry, with its story of war; the

mummers are in full glee, with bells and dance, tabor (a small drum) and pipe, and with holly garnish and sounding horn. This depiction is referenced from an article accompanying the illustration in the December 22, 1866 issue of *The Illustrated London News*.

In Miss Baker's *Glossary*, published in 1854, she describes the mummers, generally six or eight, who, during the Christmas holidays, starting on St. Thomas's Eve (December 20th), travel into rural areas and perform a burlesque tragedy at houses where they expected to be rewarded with food and drink.

Christmas Mummers
from The Illustrated London News, *December 21, 1861*
By A. Hunt

Minstrels, who added music to the celebrations, some-times accompanied them.

The following is excerpted from the article in *The Illustrated London News:*

In a beautiful manuscript in the Bodleian Library, written and illuminated in the reign of Edward III, are some spirited figures of mummers wearing the heads of animals among which the stag with branching horns is most prominent. Some of the heads are very grotesque, and remind one of the strange head-masks worn in the opening of pantomimes in the present day

[1866]. The olden performance seems to have consist-ed chiefly in dancing, and the mummers were usually attended by the minstrels, playing upon different kinds of musical instruments.

The Puritans of England did not celebrate Christmas; after all there was no reference to Christmas celebrations in the Bible. They also believed it to have had too many pagan roots. When the Puritans came to colonize America, they prohibit-ed any form of celebration of the Christmas season. In fact, in Massachusetts in 1659 they passed a law that

Christmas in New England-Colonial Times
from Harper's Weekly, *December 25, 1875*

fined anyone caught trying to participate in Christmas in any way. However, this law was rescinded twenty-two years later, but it was not until the nineteenth century that New Englanders started celebrating Christmas. Up until then the real seasonal celebration was on New Year's. With the exception, of course, of the German immigrants who celebrated Christmas in America as they did in their native Germany, on December 25th.

The Puritan in the *Harper's Weekly,* December 1875 illustration of "Christmas in New England" is admon-ishing the children for gathering holly for the pagan Christmas tradition. Gathering holly dates back to the Roman Empire when the Romans gave holly and other evergreens to friends as gifts during the Saturnalia festival. The Druids, high priests of the Celts of northern Europe, also held it as sacred during the winter solstice. It stood for never-ending life.

In *The Illustrated London News* illustration of "No Christmas" the town crier is going through the villages announcing the formal prohibition of Christmas in England.

"No Christmas" A Puritan Prohibition of Junketings
from The Illustrated London News, *December 29, 1906*
By R. Caton Woodville

During the time of Puritan influence on the non-celebration of Christmas there was a slow decline in these festivities in England, which carried over to the American colonies. The eighteenth century slipped by with little mention of the celebrating of Christmas, especially in the New England area of the United States. However, the nineteenth century brought change.

In England, the early nineteenth century started opening eyes to Christmas celebrations. By mid-century, Queen Victoria of England made her own contribution when she revived the Christmas festivities with her husband Prince Albert's German custom of the Christmas tree in 1841. However, it was the book *A Christmas Carol*, authored by Charles Dickens in 1843 (written in the span of a few months), that greatly enhanced the joyful celebration of Christmas among the English people, and thus it was transferred to America. *A Christmas Carol* changed a penny-pinching old crank (Scrooge) into a kind, thoughtful member of society.

In America this book added to the Christmas festivities along with the 1809 book *A History of New York* by Washington Irving (of *Rip Van Winkle* fame) and Clement C. Moore's 1822 poem "A Visit of St. Nicholas." These literary works were responsible for transferring the winter season's celebration from New Year's to Christmas.

In his book, Irving mentions St. Nicholas over twenty times. Although he describes him more as a Dutch gentleman with Flemish trunk hose, a low broad-brimmed hat, and a long Dutch clay pipe, Irving brought St. Nicholas, the gift giver of the Christmas season, to the forefront of the winter celebration. Likewise, Clement C. Moore's 1822 poem "A Visit of St. Nicholas," which starts out "Twas the night before Christmas" definitely intended to put the holiday celebration at Christmas not New Year's. Until this time, the predominant winter observance was New Year's. New Year's Eve had been America's time for exchanging gifts because of the Puritan objection to Christmas celebrations. Before this period Santa Claus was a part of New Years. The Germans, especially in Pennsylvania,

Charles Dickens
from Charles Dickens Rare Print Collection, n. d.
Engraved by R. Graves from Maclise's famous portrait

were calling their gift giver Kris Kringle, a derivative of Christkindel (the Christ child in German). They had been celebrating Christmas on December 25th.

One of the earliest mentions of Christmas in America was when Captain John Smith wrote that he had celebrated Christmas near the first permanent English colony of Jamestown in 1608. Jamestown was settled in 1607, before the Pilgrims made their famous landing in Massachusetts. Jamestown was on the banks of the James River in what is now Virginia. Virginia was a state that did not assimilate the Puritan influence.

The illustration "Christmas in Old Virginia" shows the festivities of the holiday season in the latter half of the nineteenth century, as does the illustration of the southern eggnog party. In early America, thick drinks

Tiny Tim and Bob Cratchit on Christmas Day (*from* A Christmas Carol) *from* Scribner's Monthly Magazine, *December 1910*
By Jessie Willcox Smith

Christmas in the South-Eggnog Party
from Harper's Weekly, *December 31, 1870*
By W. L. Sheppard

were called "grog." Eggnog was originally called "egg and grog." Others say that strong beer drinking was referred to as "noggin," so perhaps that is how it ended up being called eggnog.

In the Southwest of the United States, including California, Spanish traditions influenced Christmas festivities. The children loved the tradition of the piñata, which consisted of an earthenware container, decorated in the form of an animal, star, etc. It was hung from the ceiling and contained sweets and tiny gifts. The children, blindfolded, hit the piñata with sticks until it was broken and the contents fell to the ground. Each child scrambled to get his or her share.

Christmas on the American frontier was a very noisy time, as it was in the south. The rural settlers shot their guns into the air to wish their neighbors a "Merry Christmas." The small towns were a potpourri of foreign Christmas customs with a lot of revelry. Those were rough times in rough places.

"Christmas Morning in Old New York" appears as if it takes place around the turn of the nineteenth century. References to Christmas were seldom mentioned before the American Revolution, and Christmas celebrations weren't greatly recognized until the middle of the nineteenth century. However, New Amsterdam or New York City was settled by the Dutch Protestants

Christmas in Old Virginia
from Graphic, *December 25, 1880*
By E. A. Abbey

not the Dutch Catholics, contrary to Irving's book *A History of New York*, and they probably brought with them the celebration of Christmas on December 25th.

Goblins, witches, and ghosts have always been the essence of Halloween. But, unless you have studied the history of the Christmas season, you probably wouldn't have realized that ghosts used to be a part of Christmases past, especially on Christmas Eve. This was the night when the evil spirits were kept at bay and not allowed to do any harm.

It was believed that during this time "the cock crowed all night long" on Christmas Eve to celebrate Christ's birth, thus scaring away the evil spirits. It was

Marcellus from Shakespeare's *Hamlet* who said, "the bird of dawning singeth all night long: and then, they say, no spirit dares stir abroad; the nights are wholesome; then no planets strike. No fairy takes, nor witch hath power to charm, so hallowed and so gracious is the time."

On St. Thomas's Day (December 21st) church bells began ringing-in the merriment of Christmas in England. It was a sign of the season. Legends associated bell-ringing with the birth of Christ, even though churches didn't have bells until around the fifth century.

In America, caroling was not a large part of joy making until the late nineteenth century, even though carols date back as far as the fourth century. Victorian

Christmas Morning in Old New York
from Harper's Weekly, *December 25, 1880*
By Howard Pyle

A Ghost Story
from The Illustrated London News, *December 24, 1864*
By George Thomas

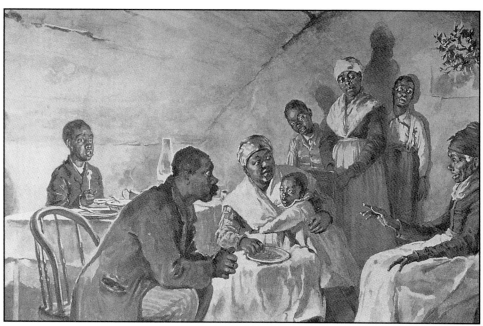

Old Aunt Sally's Christmas Eve Ghost Story
from Leslie's Weekly, *1896*
By H. Helmick

A Queen of Sheba Christmas Game
from The Illustrated London News, *December 26, 1891*

Americans enjoyed more modern carols such as "It Came upon the Midnight Clear," "Little Town of Bethlehem," and "Jingle Bells." In England waits, musicians that also patrolled the streets, walked up and down serenading house-to-house at Christmas time.

Sleigh riding was a favorite pastime among the Victorian families of the northern states. Although at times it may have been more out of a necessity than pleasure during the Christmas season. The sleigh was also used for gathering greens, including the Christmas tree, holly, and other evergreens that the Victorians loved to use to decorate their homes.

Acting a Charade Christmas Game
from The Illustrated London News, *December 24, 1869*

Blind Man's Puff a Christmas Game Well Worth the Candle *from* Graphic, *December 30, 1893* *By Sydney P. Hall*

Merrymaking at Christmas time in the nineteenth century included playing games, and the following pages include descriptions of some of those games.

Under the illustration "Blind Man's Puff," a description states that

A candle is placed somewhere with its flame about level with the player's mouth. Someone is then blindfolded, and after being turned around three or more times until dizzy or bewildered, is told to advance and blow out the candle. The victim's efforts are ludicrously misdirected. He is pulled this way and that. Finally, if ever he gets near the candle and is 'very warm,' he blows a hurricane by many points of the compass in a wrong direction and almost cracks his cheeks with futile effort.

Getting Ready for Santa Claus Christmas Eve
from Harper's Weekly, *December 30, 1876*

Christmas Presents
from Harper's Weekly, *December 30, 1865. By S. Eytinge*

Young Folks Celebrating Christmas in the South
from Harper's Weekly, *December 31, 1870*

The Christmas observances of the past were much like they are today. On Christmas Eve the children were all waiting for Santa and trying to pass the time with fun and games. Hanging stockings on the fireplace was also a large part of Christmas Eve.

Christmas morn' was always an exciting time, playing with all the new presents from the old gift giver. It was the tradition of southerners to celebrate the beginning of Christmas day with noise making, from setting off firecrackers to the shooting of guns.

The Christmas Cracker has never been as popular in America as it has been in England. It was invented by Thomas Smith in 1847. It started out as a "bon-bon" in a twist of tissue paper, which he had bought on a trip to Paris in 1840.

Tom Smith started with the "bon-bon" in twisted paper in his confectionary shop. It was very popular that Christmas but the sales dropped off after the new year. So he added a little romantic saying within the wrapper, this increased sales again. Within seven years he ended up with a little cardboard tube containing gifts of a paper hat, a tiny toy, a saying or joke, and a balloon. Smith then wrapped the whole thing with colorful paper twisted at both ends. Finally, he added a chemical that made it snap and pop when two people pulled on each end of the twist and pulled it apart. Legend has it that Smith thought of this idea one evening when he watched the log in his fireplace crackle and spark when prodded with a poker. Thus, the Christmas Cracker was born.

Snow-Balling Christmas Eve
from The Illustrated London News, *December 22, 1860*

More Explosions Expected
from The Illustrated London News, *December 23, 1893, by A. Forestier*

Vintage postcard, printed in Germany, ca. 1912

Vintage postcard, New Year Card marked Series No. 26, postally used 1911

Hearty Christmas Greeting

May Christmas bring you all the joys
That you are looking for
Sweetmeats and cake, also of toys
Quite an abundant store.

R. F.

Vintage postcard signed Ellen H. Clapsaddle
International Art Publ. Co., ca. 1910

Feasting

Christmas in the Jungle
from Graphic, *Christmas Number 1878*

In Christmases of yesteryear, great preparation went into the feasting on Christmas day. The Christmas dinner was the climax of the festivities of that grand celebration. A verse from a centuries old ballad (author unknown) goes:

The cooks shall be busied, by day and by night
In roasting and boiling, for taste and delight
Their senses in liquor that's nappy they'll steep,
Though they may be afforded to have little sleep;
They still are employed for to dress us, in brief,
Plum pudding, goose, capon, minced pies, and roast beef.

The feasting of the Yuletide season dates back to the Vikings. They held large banquets in honor of their god, Thor. Through the centuries the tradition continued in kings' castles, baronial halls, tradesmen's homes, and the peasants' dwellings.

A 1881 article accompanying the illustration of "Bob Cratchit's Christmas Dinner" in *Harper's Weekly* states: "It is worthwhile, as a preparation for Christmas, to recall that dinner at the Cratchit's, where the feasting was great, though there was only a goose for dinner, with a small pudding to follow it, while 'two tumblers and a custard cup without a handle' constituted the

Bob Cratchit's Christmas Dinner
from Harper's Weekly, *December 31, 1881*
By E. A. Abbey

A Critical Moment for the Christmas Dinner *from* Harper's Weekly, *December 1903, by E. M. Ashe*

CHRISTMAS GREETING.

Ring in, ring in the revelries,
And let the feast be one
Where not a single guest there is
But Innocence and Fun!
Let Christmas warmth keep Winter out
And Joy unbroken reign—
From floor to roof-tree send the shout
Till Christmas rings again!!

COPYRIGHT.

*Vintage Christmas card
ca. 1900*

Vintage postcard
Made in Germany, postally used 1909

whole family display of glass when the drinking of toasts began." Let us all count our blessings.

The main meat of the Christmas dinner has varied over the centuries. The "boar's head" was brought in with great ceremony to the dining chambers of castles and the tables of baronial halls. It was carried on a silver tray by the master cook, garnished with bay and rosemary with a roasted apple in its mouth.

Swans were eaten in many grand households during the sixteenth century. Peacocks were also consumed in centuries past. In T. N. Foulis's edition of *The Old English Christmas*, by Washington Irving, a footnote states:

The peacock was anciently in great demand for stately entertainments. Sometimes it was made into a pie, at one end of which the head appeared above the crust, in all its plumage, with the beak richly gilt; at the other end the tail was displayed. Such pies were served up at the solemn banquets of chivalry, when knights—errant pledged themselves to undertake any perilous enterprise, when came the ancient oath used by Justice Swallow, "by cock and pie."

According to T. G. Crippen's *Christmas and Christmas Lore*, "'The Roast Beef of Old England' was great Christmas fare." Crippen went on to say it was "a baron

Bringing In the Boar's Head
from The Illustrated London News, *December 22, 1855, by J. Gilbert*

The Pride of the Christmas Feast
from Harper's Weekly, *December 26, 1885*
By C. Y. Turner

from The Old English Christmas, n.d., *by Washington Irving*
Book illustration by H. M. Brock

Alexandra's Feast
from Punch, or the London Charivari, December 24, 1902

The Christmas Chariot—The Coming of the Plum Pudding
from Harper's Weekly, January 1, 1876

of beef, i.e. two sirloins, not cut asunder, but joined by the end of the backbone." Other popular meats used through the years include turkey, goose, pig, mutton, capons, venison, and even goat with pudding in its belly.

The minced pie of long ago, more aptly called "the Christmas pie" was greatly attached to the holiday feast. In the seventeenth century, according to *Christmastide, Its History, Festivities, and Carols*, by William Sandys, the minced pies consisted of "neat's tongues (ox, cow, etc.), chicken, eggs, sugar, currants, lemon and orange peel with various spices."

Sandys continues by saying that a later recipe included not meat but "a pound of beef suet, chopped fine; a pound of raisins, stoned; a pound of currants cleaned dry; a pound of apples chopped fine; two or

three eggs; allspice beat very fine, and sugar to your taste; a little salt; and as much brandy and wine as you like."

An old English saying or superstition declared—in as many houses as you eat a minced pie during the twelve days of Christmas, so many happy months you will have in the New Year.

Charles II may have brought plum pudding, an eighteenth century term for the old plum porridge, to the forefront of the English Christmas dinner. It has never thrived in such a manner, however, outside of England.

A typical plum pudding consisted of suet, raisins, currants, eggs, flour, salt, cinnamon and nutmeg with a little brandy or wine. Then it was wrapped in cloth and boiled in a large pan of water for several hours. The plums in plum pudding had vanished before the early

Making the Christmas Pudding
from The Illustrated London News, *Christmas 1848*
By Kenny Meadows

Taking Up the Christmas Pudding
from The Illustrated London News, *Christmas 1848*
By Kenny Meadows

Guarding the Christmas Pie
from The Illustrated London News, *Christmas Number 1909*
By Gordon Robinson

Seasonable Cheer
from The Illustrated London News, *December 27, 1879*
By *Valentine Bromley*

Vintage postcard
Postally used 1909

Vintage postcard
Postally used 1910

1800s for reasons unknown.

Plum pudding came attached to an old superstition that every person in the household had to share in the stirring of the pudding or else the family would not prosper.

At sunset on January 6th or Epiphany, there was a great celebration. Originally the festivities were in honor of the day the magi presented the Christ child with their gifts of gold, frankincense, and myrrh. This was called the Twelfth Night (twelve days after Christmas) and a great feast was held. A large cake was brought to the feast with a bean and a pea baked inside. Whoever received the bean was named king of the night's celebration, and the person with the pea was named queen. If the wrong sex received the bean or pea, they appointed someone to the honor. Heavy drinking and other merrymaking ensued for the rest of the evening.

Stirring the Christmas Pudding
from The Illustrated London
News, *December 21, 1889*
By M. Brown

Christmas in the Fields
from source unknown, n.d.
By John S. Davis

The King of the Bean
from The Illustrated London News, *December 19, 1857*
By Edmond Morin

In *Christmas and Christmas Lore,* T. G. Crippen states that a mock court of characters was set up for the evening. The characters were written on slips of paper and drawn from a hat, which was the English custom in the time of Charles II. Later these were courtly, historical, or legendary characters taken from the popular comedies of the day.

On Epiphany or Twelfth Night in nineteenth century Normandy, France there was a custom involving the Twelfth Night cake. After the family dinner, the cake was brought in, already sliced into equal portions. The youngest member of the family handed out the pieces. The first piece was called "the good God's share" and was given to the poor. On this night the poor would go from door-to-door collecting generous donations of money.

The second share or piece went to the absent member of the family and was placed aside in a cupboard. It

Christmas Time—Feeding the Pets
from Harper's Weekly, *December 31, 1870, by A. E. Emslie*

The Christmas Sheaf
from Harper's Bazaar, *January 29, 1870*

Stirring the Christmas Pudding
from Graphic, *Christmas Number 1881*
By Henry Woods

was used by the family as a barometer of the missing person's health. The mother of the family would look at it from time-to-time and according to the state of preservation of the cake, knew whether the missing person was in good or bad health. If the cake was a little mildewed it was thought to be a bad sign.

The remaining pieces were given to whomever the youngest member of the family chose. The lucky one to get the bean was named the King or Queen for the night. Every time he or she took a drink of spirits, deafening shouts were heard. Generally the royalty took

good care to make them shout as often as he or she could, making the evening pass merrily.

The Victorians were always concerned with the feeding of the animals and birds at Christmas time, therefore, extra feed was always provided.

In Norway and Sweden, according to the article that accompanied the illustration "The Christmas Sheaf," the last sheaf from the harvest field was never threshed; it was always carefully reserved, both by the rich and the poor, till Christmas Eve. The article goes on to state,

The Twelfth Night Cake
from source unknown
Book illustration, ca. 1900

Vintage postcard, printed in Germany
Postally used 1909

On that evening it is brought out and fastened to a pole, and set up in front of the dwelling or on the roof as a feast for the hungry little birds. The inhabitants of the household then partake of their supper—a family feast for which the utmost ingenuity is exercised in providing the greatest variety of cakes, etc. One of each sort is apportioned to every one in the house, including all the servants. A Swedish lady says; 'these, with many other customs, are most strictly observed even by the poorest peasant. My father's sheaf is always set up every Christmas Eve, and it is a most beautiful sight to see the little birds of every kind flocking to and feasting on the Christmas sheaf.'

Vintage postcard, International Art Publ. Co., ca. 1910

Good Old Santa Claus

Vintage postcard, S. Bergman
Postally used 1915

You might call St. Nicholas, who was the bishop of Myra, the first Santa Claus. He lived in what is now Turkey and came to prominence throughout Europe by the tenth century. St. Nicholas became the patron saint of many groups including sailors, pawnbrokers, and children. He is also the patron saint of Russia.

He visited many children in Europe on his feast day, December 6th, or the eve before, especially in the Netherlands. St. Nicholas, in centuries past, questioned the children on their knowledge of the Bible. For the correct answers, the children were rewarded with fruit, nuts, and sweets. Sometimes he traveled with a donkey or a white horse or simply on foot. In some countries the old saint traveled with an assistant and/or angels to help with the children.

In the illustration "Grand Welcome to Santa Claus by the Children of All Nations" the children of the world are welcoming Santa of America. The traditional Santa, as we know him today, wasn't quite established before the end of the nineteenth century. It was not until artist Haddon Sundblom came up with his Coca-Cola® Santa in the 1930s that our vision of Santa was firmly imbedded in our minds.

In England Father Christmas was also called King Christmas, Old Christmas, and Mr. Christmas. He was previously mentioned in the section on Christmas masque's of old England.

The Punch magazine depicted many cartoons of Father Christmas. In the illustration "The Wassail Bowl," he is bringing the wassail bowl of peace and goodwill to the

Vintage postcard marked SB 3118 N
Belgium, postally used 1912

St. Nicholas, Victorian die cut, ca. 1900

Grand Welcome to Santa Claus by the Children of All Nations
from Frank Leslie's Illustrated Newspaper, *Christmas Number 1886*

The Weihnachtsman in Pomerania
from German Magazine Illustration, *ca. 1900*

people of the world. In old England he was usually wearing a wreath of evergreens around his head.

One of Germany's gift givers was called the Weihnachtsman or the Christmas man. "The Weihnachtsman" is a depiction of the Weihnachtsman receiving gifts for the children from the angels.

In the Pomeranian region of Germany the Christmas man and his entourage rewarded only the well-behaved children. Dressed in animal disguises, helpers frequently accompanied the Weihnachtsman, and quite often frightened the children. In some areas the Christmas man was also joined by St. Nicholas.

Christmas is Coming
from Punch, *or the* London Charivari, *December 24, 1892*

The Wassail Bowl
from Punch, *or the* London Charivari, *December 29, 1888*

The Weihnachtsman
from German Magazine Illustration, *1897*

How King Christmas Comes
from Graphic, *Christmas Number 1921*
By E. B. Bernard

All the Fault of the Wright Brothers
from source unknown, ca. 1920
By Harry Grant Dart

King Christmas drops in to visit the children on December 25th in the early part of the aviation age.

The Wright brothers were blamed for the occasional disaster of Santa's arrival at Christmas.

Traditional depictions of Santa were well on their way to being formed at the turn of the twentieth century, especially in books of the period.

Many well-known illustrators of the early twentieth

Vintage poster
ca 1900

from Twas the Night Before Christmas
Book illustration, ca. 1900

from Twas the Night Before Christmas
Book illustration, ca. 1910

century painted Santa. In "Santa Claus Preparing for His Annual Visit," Norman Price shows Santa gathering his toys for the long journey.

On the cover of the December 1914 issue of *Judge Magazine,* by artist James Montgomery Flagg, a traditional-looking Santa is being led by cupid. Flagg is

from Santa Claus and His Works
Book cover, McLoughlin Bros., 1897

from Santa Claus Story Book
Book cover, M. A. Donohue & Co., 1913

The Universal Santa Claus
from Judge Magazine, *December 1900*
By V. Gillam

The Court of King Christmas the Only Crowned Head to Whom
Uncle Sam Takes Off His Hat, *from* The Christmas Puck, *n.d.*
By T. Keppler

from Judge Magazine, *December 5, 1914*
Cover by James Montgomery Flagg

well-known for his World War I recruiting poster, "I Want You," of Uncle Sam.

In the English cartoon, by T. Keppler, Uncle Sam takes off his hat to King Christmas of England.

Uncle Sam was portrayed as Santa Claus in many cartoons of the late nineteenth and early twentieth century. He delivered his gifts to U.S. presidents and countries of Europe.

Nothing For Grover (Cleveland) This Year
from Judge Magazine, *December 29, 1894*
By V. Gillam

Santa Claus Preparing for His Annual Visit
from St. Nicholas Magazine, ca. 1912
By Norman Price

Vintage postcard
Printed in Germany, ca. 1910

Christmas Postcard Era
1900-1940

A Peaceful Christmas

Vintage postcard marked PFB Serie 11000
Printed in Germany, ca. 1910

Vintage postcard
Postally used 1904

Vintage postcard
Made in Germany, postally used 1907

It should be mentioned that postcard enthusiasts referred to the years between 1898 and 1918 as the "Golden Age of Postcards." Germany produced most of these cards, and the Germans were greatly admired for their artistic renderings of these beautiful depictions.

On early Christmas postcards, usually those before 1907, senders wrote messages on the front of the card. Additional text on the back of the card was not allowed, by order of the post office, because this space was provided for the address only.

Vintage postcard marked PFB No. 9440 Relief, No. 9441 Brilliant, printed in Germany, ca.1910

Vintage postcard Dated 1909

During the Christmas postcard era beautifully rendered religious-themed Christmas postcards became popular. The Holy family was shown either as a group or with baby Jesus depicted alone or with his mother, the Virgin Mary.

May Christmas bring you Peace.

Vintage postcard signed C. M. Burd
Ernest Nister
Printed in Bavaria, ca. 1912

Vintage postcard
Czechoslovakia, postally used 1933

The Magi trekked their way, guided by the Christmas Star, and reached the baby Jesus on January 6th (Epiphany). They then presented their gifts of gold, frankincense, and myrrh to the Christ child.

A merry Christmas to You

Vintage postcard
Printed in Germany, dated 1908

Vintage postcard
Printed in Germany, postally used 1912

Vintage postcard marked Serie 1480
Printed in Germany, postally used 1910

Gorgeous Christmas postcards from Germany pictured baby Jesus being watched over by adoring guardian angels.

Many Christmas postcards depicted baby Jesus as a young child delivering the presents and Christmas tree with the help of assistants.

There were also numerous angel Christmas postcards in circulation at the beginning of the twentieth century.

Vintage postcard
Made in Czechoslovakia, postally used ca. 1940

Vintage postcard signed P. Ebner, ca. 1912

Vintage postcard marked Serie 127
Printed in Germany, ca. 1910

Vintage postcard, Christmas Postcard No. 8263
Raphael Tuck & Sons, postally used ca. 1910

Vintage postcard marked 928/31
Printed in Germany, ca. 1910

Vintage postcard marked B. W. 298
Printed in Germany, ca. 1909

Vintage postcard marked S & L Co. N 1321
Printed in Germany, ca. 1910

On some Christmas postcards, angels were illustrated carrying the Christmas tree.

On others, angels brought the gifts in the name of the Christ child.

Many of the Christmas postcards created by German artists were of angels adorned with a crown, a star, or a halo.

Vintage postcard
Printed in Germany, ca. 1909

Vintage postcard
Printed in Germany, postally used 1915

Vintage postcard marked S B 2169 N
Netherlands, ca. 1908

Vintage postcard marked PFB No. 8935 Relief, No. 8937 Gel Printed in Germany, postally used ca. 1910

Vintage postcard
Austria, postally used ca. 1910

Depictions of Santa Claus were also popular during this time. St. Nicholas usually brought his presents to the "good" children on the eve of his feast day, December 6th. He is still greatly celebrated in the Netherlands today.

*Vintage postcard
ca. 1908*

Vintage postcard
Printed in Saxony, ca. 1910

Vintage postcard marked E.C.C. Serie 55/56
Printed in Germany, ca. 1908

Many of the German generated Santa postcards for the American market depicted German-looking gift givers. Quite often these Santas were shown carrying switches for the "bad" children.

A MERRY CHRISTMAS

Vintage postcard
Made in Germany, postally used 1908

Vintage postcard marked 1249
Printed in Germany, ca. 1910

Vintage postcard
Postally used 1912

Vintage postcard marked Dessin 12 No. 15938
Printed in Germany, postally used 1910

Vintage postcard marked Series 522 A
Made in U.S.A., ca. 1916

We are more familiar with the traditional look of Santa Claus in America.

However, the appearance of gift givers throughout Europe is distinctly different from the American Santa figure.

Vintage postcard
ca. 1910

Vintage postcard marked Serie 7500
Postally used 1923

Vintage postcard
Hungary, postally used 1923

Vintage postcard
Poland, postally used 1911

Vintage postcard
Germany, postally used 1914

Vintage postcard
Russia, dated 1921

Vintage postcard
ca. 1910

According to Clement C. Moore's poem "A Visit of St. Nicholas," it reads "And I heard him exclaim, as he drove out of sight, Happy Christmas to all and to all a good night."

Vintage postcard
Suhling & Koehn Co.
Printed in Germany, postally used 1908

Along with religious icons and Santa, postcards also illustrated the symbols of Christmas. The Christmas candle represents the Light of the World, Jesus Christ.

The Christmas Star led the Magi to the Christ child. Bells, according to legends, rang when Christ was born.

Vintage postcard marked PFB Serie 6985
Printed in Germany, postally used 1908

Vintage postcard marked No 1000
International Art Publ. Co., printed in Germany, postally used 1907

Vintage postcard
Postally used 1912

Secular symbols of Christmas include the Christmas tree, the stocking, and the poinsettia. Many people believe the custom of the tree came from Germany. There is no actual proof it did, but it is widely accepted as being so (see *Christmas Past*).

Vintage postcard
Printed in Germany, postally used 1909

The stocking was brought to the forefront by Clement C. Moore's poem. Some historians believe the custom of the stocking goes back to the story about St. Nicholas, the Bishop of Myra, presenting gifts to the daughters of his friend (see also *Christmas Past*).

DESIGN COPYRIGHTED, JOHN WINSCH, 1912.

Vintage postcard
Postally used 1912

The poinsettia was brought to prominence by Joel Poinsett. He was the first U.S. ambassador to Mexico. Ambassador Poinsett found this plant growing along the roadside in Mexico in 1828 and brought it to the United States.

A Merry Christmas.

Painting Copyright 1912 by Frances Brundage.

Vintage postcard, Postcard Series No. 208, signed Frances Brundage Printed in Germany, ca. 1912

Vintage postcard
ca. 1915

Portrayals of children were always adored by the early twentieth century collectors of Christmas postcards. These images of merry children warmed the hearts of many and were a loving addition to scrapbooks.

A Merry Christmas.

Vintage postcard, Christmas Series Postcard No. 204
Printed in Germany, postally used 1911

Vintage postcard signed Ellen H. Clapsaddle
Printed in Germany, postally used 1909

Vintage postcard
Printed in Germany, ca. 1912

Vintage postcard marked PFB Serie 9055
Printed in Germany, postally used 1909

A merry CHRISTMAS

650

Vintage postcard
Postally used 1906

Vintage postcard marked PFB No. 5418 Relief, No. 5416 Relief
m. Goldtieldruck
ca. 1908

Vintage postcard
Raphael Tuck & Sons
Printed in Saxony, postally used 1908

Many children were shown with a guardian angel. According to the Bible, God has angels watching over the little ones. Everyone has a guardian angel (see Matthew 18:10).

Vintage postcard
Ernest Nister
Printed in Bavaria, postally used 1907

Elves were very much a part of the Christmas tradition in Scandinavian countries. In Sweden they were called the Jultomten. The Jultomten would knock on the door on Christmas Eve and yell "Are there any good children in this house?" If there was an affirmative response they would deliver the presents. In Norway and Denmark the elves were called the Julenisse. However, in Denmark they did not deliver presents. In Finland the elves were called the tontut.

Vintage postcard
Ernest Nister
Printed in Bavaria, ca. 1907

Vintage postcard marked 4225/8
Sweden, ca. 1920

Vintage postcard
Sweden, postally used 1915

In all Scandinavian countries, families would leave the elves a good supper on Christmas Eve of porridge and a drink of milk or beer. This kept the elves happy; therefore, they wouldn't wreak havoc in the homes in the coming year. The elves were responsible for taking care of the homes, farm buildings, and the animals. If the animals were mistreated by their owners, the elves could cause the families to suffer from bad health and many accidents.

*Vintage postcard marked Serie 163, signed by G. Stoopendaal
Sweden, postally used 1914*

*Vintage postcard signed by Jenny Nyström
Sweden, ca. 1910*

Vintage postcard marked Series 2790
International Art Publ. Co.
ca. 1910

Vintage postcard
Meissner & Buch
Germany, ca. 1920

We will end this book with snowmen, which were often used on postcards for Christmas and New Year's.

They are still collectible today as are all of the wonderful postcards in *Christmas Merrymaking*.

Viel Glück im neuen Jahre

Vintage postcard
Mailed in Austria, postally used 1932

Best wishes for a merry CHRISTMAS

Vintage postcard
Printed in Germany, ca. 1912

A MERRY CHRISTMAS to you

Vintage postcard
Made in Germany, ca. 1912

SELECTED RESOURCES GUIDE

Imagery of vintage Christmas postcards, book, magazine and newspaper illustrations, and engravings from 1848 to around 1940 are from the author's Christmas ephemera collection. All photography of imagery is by the author.

Numerous articles in newspapers of the nineteenth century that accompanied the illustrations were used as sources as well as the books in the following list.

Christmas in Colonial and Early America. Chicago: World Book Encyclopedia, Inc., 1975.

Crippen, T. G. *Christmas and Christmas Lore.* New York: The Dodge Publishing Co., 1928. Reprint, Detroit: Omnigraphics, 1990.

Hervey, Thomas K. *The Book of Christmas.* Boston: Roberts Brothers, 1888.

Irving, Washington. *Diedrich Knickerbocker's History of New York.* New York: The Heritage Press, 1940.

_____. *The Old English Christmas.* London & Edinburgh: T. N. Foulis, n.d.

Restad, Penne L. *Christmas in America: A History.* New York: Oxford University Press, 1995.

Sandys, William. *Christmastide, Its History, Festivities, and Carols.* London: John Russell Smith, n.d.

Vintage postcard
Printed in Germany, postally used ca. 1912

Vintage postcard, Christmas Postcards Series No.136 Raphael Tuck & Sons ca. 1912